GODS AND MEN

WENDY POWELL LEWIS

Sachs New York Publishing

Sachs New York Publishing

GODS AND MEN

WENDY POWELL LEWIS

Sachs New York Publishing

Canada Offices
237 St Vincent Street
Meaford, Ontario
N4L 1C1 Canada

CONTACT PUBLISHER
Gough Lewis, Director of Sachs New York Publishing
Email: GoughLewis@gmail.com
#519-538-1519

ISBN: 978-0-9813306-3-1

Sachs New York Publishing

GODS AND MEN

WENDY POWELL LEWIS

Illustrated by Steele Savage

Sachs New York Publishing

To my reader

CONTENTS

Acknowledgments

I would like to acknowledge the help I received from the following books:

Graves, Robert. *The Greek Myths I & II*. Folio Society, 2001

Hamilton, Edith. *Mythology*. Little Brown, 1942

Homer. *The Odyssey*. Translated by Robert Fitzgerald, Anchor Books, 1963

Homer. *The Odyssey*. Translated by E.V. Rieu. Penguin Classics Edition, 1946

Homer. *The Odyssey*. Translated by Walter Shewring, Oxford University Press, 1986

Foreword

My renewed interest in the Greek myths could have been inspired by the documentary series *Ancient Aliens* as shown on the History Channel. The proposition that extraterrestrials visited planet Earth many years ago, and influenced the development of mankind and the course of human history, is not only intriguing, but also worthy of the scientific studies now being applied to it.

Big questions rise like monoliths. We ask: Who were the gods? Were they more than inventions, more than figments of the imagination? Could they have been extraterrestrials with advanced technology whose powers made them appear god-like? The questions provide avenues of thought as astonishing as the Nazca lines of Peru, or the megalithic stones of Puma Punku in Bolivia.

For my purposes, however, and for the writing of this book, I have explored the Greek myths as they have been handed down to us. The time frame is about two thousand years B.C. (it could be earlier) to fifth century A.D. when Aeschylus wrote his plays about Atreus' descendants. I did not set out to unify the tales, yet links emerged, names re-appeared, so did unifying themes.

I begin with Odysseus in his field in Ithaca, and from there, I follow the trail of my impulses. The Trojan War takes central position, because it affects, to some degree, every character I write about. In the last poem, I return to the House of Atreus, a House burdened by its past and hated by the gods. In this poem, we learn, with Orestes, why his House is defiled. The iniquity of the fathers is visited upon the children, in this case, unto the third generation. The theme is vengeance. Apollo makes it clear to Orestes that he must avenge his father's death. It is his fate and obligation.

"... ye shall be as gods, knowing good and evil."

Bible, Genesis 3.5

Breaking Cover

In the first place
Odysseus did not want to go to war
It was an interruption

He had work to do in his own kingdom
His island was a better place when he was home
People strove and felt protected

The chief away
Meant they were open to the winds and to the sky
Tossed on a breaking sea

In truth, home was the place to be
With his little child and Penelope
And his aging father Laertes

But his peace was cleft in two
The day the dark ship docked
And three men came walking

Trouble had come to his shore
And he was forced to recall
The court of Tyndareus

The pledge the chieftains had made
That fateful day
And what they had bargained for

Standing on pieces of horse flesh
In the yard that ran with blood
Swearing to unite

And defend the rights
Of the suitor who was chosen
Should Helen of Troy be stolen

It was a pledge of his own devising
Which had come back to haunt him
Returned to ensnare him!

But not yet, not quite
He would feign madness
He would don a peasant's cap

Pretend he did not know
Agamemnon, Menelaus and Palamedes
The three men who came walking

He would plow the field
An ox yoked to an ass
Sow salt instead of seed

And that was how they found him
But Palamedes with a mind
Like a swordbreaker

Seized Odysseus's little son
Threw him before the plow
And Odysseus turned the plow aside

To save his child
And in so doing, broke his cover
Gave the child back to his mother

His ruse had been discovered
Odysseus knew what was in store
Helen of Sparta had been stolen

He was bound to go to war
Now there was only one holdout
And Odysseus offered to rout him out

He was the one no war could do without
Achilles, greatest warrior of them all
Taught on Mount Pelion by Cheiron

Who at age six could kill a boar
Catch fawns on the run . . .
But Thetis, his mother, knew more

Knew what was in store:
If her son went to Troy
He was fated to die

She had sent him to the court of Lycomedes
Sworn to secrecy
He was draped in veils and decked in jewels

Only the maidens knew
Their lips were sealed
But their eyes gave a clue

And whispers have a way of traveling
They hang on leaves and move down streams
They cross the wind-whipped seas

On dark ships and boats they go afloat
Odysseus found whispers on the loose
Where the clothes were being sluiced

He went to the court of Lycomedes
Disguised as a peddler
With a basketful of ornaments

They made the women sigh
But what caught Achilles' eye
Were the weapons embedded in the trinkets

Swords and daggers exceedingly fine
He shoved the women aside
And in so doing, broke his cover

Odysseus threw his hat into the air
The two men laughed to see each other
Ripped off the maiden veils

Leaving shreds about the floor
They would ignore what fate had in store
They knew what they had bargained for

Achilles' mother, Thetis, heard it all
Brought her son a shield like no other
Made by Hephaestus in Olympus

It set back the event of her son's death
But his death came nonetheless
Achilles died as prophesied

Odysseus survived ten years of war
And ten years more
Before he returned to Ithaca's shore.

Clytemnestra

On the surface
It seemed like treachery
Clytemnestra the treacherous one

She saw the fire on the hillside
Knew the time had come
Rolled out the purple carpet

Welcomed Agamemnon home
Priam's daughter brought from Troy
Left outside alone

She led him to the bathhouse
Where the slave girls waited
Lavishly they cleansed him

Lathered, scrubbed, and oiled him
Then the high king rose
From his watery repose

Looking forward to the feast ahead
And his good wife with the towel came
To wrap the big man round

But Agamemnon found
Himself ensnared
Trapped in a garment made of netting

Without neck or sleeves
And Clytemnestra's hate-filled lover
Enemy of the House of Atreus

Broke his cover
Struck Agamemnon with his sword
Who tumbled back

Into the silver-sided bath
And, wanting her husband dead
Clytemnestra severed his head

Then ran out to the wife-in-all-but-name
Brought from the wars much to her shame
And wielded her axe a second time

Severed her head
And Cassandra was dead
And the ground stained red

I interject here, dear reader,
To tell you there was more
Often overlooked, that went before

It must be told
Lest judgment be distorted
And facts go unreported

Agamemnon of the House of Atreus
Richest of kings
In the Mediterranean world

Was also barbarous
He had killed
Clytemnestra's former husband

He had killed the baby at her breast
Forced her to marry him
And then had gone to war

But that was not all, dear reader
Ask the witnesses who saw
For some the sun does not rise again

For some
It does not shine on them
And will nevermore

The men were trapped at Aulis
Prisoners of winds and tides
One thousand ships and counting

Men ready to die, yet held there
Angered by their waiting
Hearts fit for breaking

They wanted nothing more
Than to carry out
What they had bargained for

Then Calchas came
To the Commander-in-Chief
And spoke his soothsayer's words:

"Artemis, daughter of Zeus, is angry
She has to be appeased
A sacrifice she will need

If you want to calm the winds
And change the tides
Your daughter young and fair

Must be laid on the altar there."
Agamemnon gasped
Clasped himself around

Turned away
Iphigenia was the joy of his house
And Clytemnestra's child

But the men had heard
The men had seen
Dark were their faces

Dark were their thoughts
They wanted the young girl dead
But it was left unsaid

Agamemnon, leader of men
On his way to Troy
Knew his warriors' minds

Knew the price of waiting
Knew they would repudiate him
If sanction were denied

"How can I bring her here?" he replied.
Cunning Odysseus stepped forward
He had a ruse for every occasion

And was skilled in the art of persuasion:
"Tell Clytemnestra you've arranged a wedding
Tell her Iphigenia is to marry Achilles

Greatest warrior of them all
And to bring her wedding dress."
Agamemnon acquiesced

He was not bound, he told himself
Like a boat tacking across the bay
He could change the course

Clytemnestra brought Iphigenia
To that place where screams
Joined with the winds and tides

Howls never heard before
Raged along the wind-lashed shore
To which Clytemnestra added more

Men crouched on the ground
Locked in their fears
And covered their ears

But Iphigenia made no sound
Silently, she went to her death
In her wedding dress

And it was said
The tide turned
The winds abated

Calchas was repudiated
A thousand ships went out to sea
Some said the sacrifice had to be

But, dear reader, I think you'll agree
That when Clytemnestra wielded her axe
And Agamemnon's head fell to the floor

When he came home from the war
He died for those he'd sacrificed
The ones that went before

Hephaestus

Hera took her newborn son
And threw him off the mountainside
Because she could not look on him with pride

It was humiliating she told herself
That the supreme god Zeus
And the supreme goddess Hera

Should have an offspring
That looked no better--
So small and ugly

It brought on mockery
Gave rise to laughter
Which found legs

Ran behind walls
Slipped into banqueting halls
Hid in the myrtle trees

But unknown to Hera
She had flung her baby wide
He did not hit the mountainside

He did not hit the rocks below
He fell into the sea
And was scooped up

By the gentle Nereids:
Thetis and Eurynome
Who took him to their grotto

And raised him lovingly
He was the baby who fell from the sky
Into the blue Aegean Sea

***

Hephaestus grew quickly
And knew early
What he wanted to be

He learned about minerals and metallurgy
By nine he had a forge of his own
He made brooches, clasps, and belts

Inlaid with the jewels of the sea
And a range of weaponry
His life was burning bright

In the grotto of the night
But it was to change suddenly
When the supreme goddess, Hera

Saw the brooch the Nereid wore
It was silver with jade at the core
And Hera wanted to know more--

Whose workmanship it was
That was good enough for a god?
And she forced an answer from her

That same day
Hera took her son away
To the place, she said, where he belonged

To Olympus high on the hill
With his father Zeus
And his mother Hera

Where her son would have a forge like no other:
Twenty bellows working day and night
He would be the element burning bright

And he became so reconciled with his mother
That he challenged his father
About his treatment of her

How Zeus had blamed her
For the rebellion of the gods
How for punishment

He had hung her in the sky
A golden bracelet at each wrist
An anvil at each ankle

And the gods had heard her cry
But they had all stood by--
They didn't want to die

They were afraid of Zeus's thunderbolt
Fatal to god and man
Then Zeus turned on his son

He did not deliver the fatal flash
He heaved him into the sky
With a strength that was his for the summoning

And for Hephaestus, it was the time again for falling
This time he did not land in the sea
He landed on the Isle of Lemnos

Broke both legs
And would have been left for dead
Had the islanders not found him

If he had been the God of War
The gods would have left him there
But he was the God of Fire

The Sorcerer of the Forge
And they needed their shields
And their swords

They needed the bellows working day and night
They needed the one who knew
The one who could do . . .

They said Zeus's anger would not last
That peace would come to pass
And it did

Hephaestus was reinstated
But he had no time to talk
He made a pair of golden leg-supports

So he could walk
He made a set of 'handmaidens' all of gold
Which followed orders--did what they were told

He made twenty, three-legged tables with golden wheels
Which could come and go as their inventor pleased.
For Europa, daughter of King Sidon, he made

A basket of fine gold mesh chased with figuring
Showing Io after she was changed into a heifer
And all the incidents of her suffering

At the hands of Zeus because he was licentious
At the hands of Hera because she was so jealous
And Hera called herself "the protectress"!

He made a shield for Thetis to give to Achilles
Because the Nereid had rescued him from the sea
And raised him lovingly

***

But the time came when Hephaestus
Married the Goddess of Love and Beauty
Aphrodite, born of the foam

Whom every god wanted for his own
But she was known for her infidelities
This time it was Ares, God of War

Hephaestus found them in the marriage bed
Made by his hands with love and trembling
And he trapped them under a hunting net

Unbreakable yet fine as lace
Hammered out of bronze
And locked in place

He called for the gods to bear witness
To come to the scene of his shame
He called for the return of the marriage gifts

Extorted by Zeus, the Extorter
Who, according to Hera, his mother,
Was his wife's adoptive father

And the couple lay trapped for all to see
Under the fine bronze filigree
Ares shouting angrily

Aphrodite laughing sweetly and mockingly
Flirting under the lace made of bronze
And Hermes wanted to marry her

And Poseidon too
He wanted to pay the debt
Get under the net

Gag the God of War
Give him no quarter
Put him in Promethean chains

Send maggots to eat his brains
Some said Hephaestus smiled
Some said he almost laughed

"Life has its pains," was the gods' jocular claim
But there was nothing further to be gained
So Hephaestus unlocked the hunting net

And naked Ares fled
As if Cerberus were on his heels
His three mouths slobbering

All his teeth revealed
And the gods were inclined to roar
At anything to do with the God of War

They said Hephaestus had won
That in his moment of shame
His triumph had reigned.

***

Aphrodite expressed no regret
But urged by Hera, her mother-in-law,
She went to Paphos

As was the custom
And bathed there in the sea
Thus restoring her virginity

And when she returned in all her radiance
Put her arms around him
Told him he was The One

Hephaestus knew what to do
He took her in his Herculean arms
To where the myrtle trees grew

And a small zephyr blew
And golden birds sang golden songs
And all seemed beautiful and true

The Judgment of Paris

The child was the second son of Hecube
Handsomest of all Priam's fifty sons
Born with a warning over his head

That he would ruin Troy
He was given to a herdsman
Agelaus by name

Who took him to Mount Ida
But when the time came
Agelaus could not find the will to kill

He left the babe in a grassy hollow
Under an open sky
On the slopes of Mount Ida

A few days later, Agelaus found
The child was still alive
He saw a she-bear nearby

Assumed the bear had suckled him
How else could he have survived?
He placed the child in a soft-skinned wallet

Took him home to be raised as his own
To be a herdsman like himself
And he called the child Paris

***

When Paris was full-grown
He became the chosen one
Of the lovely nymph, Oenone

They hunted and herded together
Whispered words of love
Carved each other's names

In beech and poplar
On the favored slopes of Mount Ida
And there the story might have ended

But it was the beginning only
Because Zeus was observing earthlings
He had seen a herder of god-like beauty

And he wanted to know more
But, for the moment
He was planning a war:

How to get one started
Rolling in his hand a golden apple
With the inscription: 'For the Fairest'

He was smiling at the incendiary words
In the background was the sound of celebration
King Peleus and Thetis were getting married

Zeus had given the bride away
But he could not stay
He had been to too many weddings

He was thinking an apple with such an inscription
Could foment trouble
Beyond description

He saw Eris pacing the floor
The Goddess of Discord was angry
She had not been invited to the wedding

It was a twice-told tale and such a bore
But Zeus's mind leapt to the fore
He signaled Eris to come near

He whispered in her ear
She smiled slowly
Took the golden ball

Read the inscription: 'For the Fairest'
And rolled it into the banqueting hall
The apple was seized

An uproar began
A competition followed
Three finalists were chosen

Zeus was asked to be the judge
Cleverly, he refused
He was occupied

He was pressed for time
He had an agenda to refine
He instructed Hermes:

"Seek out the herder on Mount Gargaris
Highest peak of Mount Ida
Paris is his name

"Let Paris be the judge
Let him award the golden ball
He can make the judgment call."

***

Dazzling in form, and radiant
Three goddesses appeared on the mount
Hera, Athene, and Aphrodite

Hermes came along to explain
What it was about
But Paris had his doubts:

"How can a cattleman play this part?
They all look beautiful to me
My wish is to cut the apple in three."

Hermes said: "Zeus has spoken.
This is something you must do.
You have no choice. See it through."

"Then they should disrobe," Paris said
"How can I judge them when they are clothed?"
So the goddesses disrobed

They smiled at their predicament
Standing on the slopes
With the cows and goats

But they took it in their stride
The judge said he would see each one alone
Paris had not thought of bribes

But the goddesses came armed
With swooning smiles
And bribes that stupefied

Hera offered Asia as if it were a bauble
Athene offered untold victories in battle
Aphrodite offered Helen of Sparta

"How can you do that?" Paris exclaimed
"It can be arranged," the goddess claimed
"Helen will fall in love with you

"You will live in a palace
Servants at your door
Ships for the high seas

"Bullfights on demand
A sword in your hand
That is, if you choose me."

And Paris chose Aphrodite
He gave her the golden apple
He made the judgment call

And he made two enemies that day
Who could never be placated
And would never go away.

***

After that encounter
Paris felt restless
He wanted to leave

Go to the bullfights in Troy
"You have your own bullfights
"Isn't that enough?" Agelaus said

But it wasn't enough
Agelaus and Paris went to Troy
At the close of the sixth lap of the chariot race

The boxing match began, and the king looked on
Paris sprang into the arena and boxed his way to glory
Some said he had no skill ... courage only

But he won the crown
Then he won the footrace
And another crown

Priam's sons saw it all and wanted to kill
The upstart slave who had won two crowns
They challenged him to another footrace

They said his victories were luck, no more
A second footrace would show a true score
Tension stretched like ox hide on a shield

But Paris never thought to yield
He won again
It was his third crown of the day

But Priam's sons wanted things their way
They blocked the exits with armed guards
Hector and Deiphobus ran at him with their swords

Paris leapt to Zeus's altar for protection
Agelaus shouted: "He is your son! Great King!
Help him! Help him!"

Agelaus showed the baby's rattle
Hecube confirmed it was the child's
And the news gave Priam pause

He laid his hand upon his heart
Awed by what had come to pass
And vowed a sacrifice

But the priests still wanted Paris dead
Insisted he would ruin Troy
The priests were silenced

And King Priam turned to one and all:
"Better that Troy fall
Than I lose my son again."

***

Priam gave his son a fleet of ships
And mariners to help him sail the seas
And pushed along by a favorable breeze

Paris sailed for Sparta.
When King Priam's son arrived
The sun lay on the water

And the purple carpet rolled outside
Splendid were the gifts
He brought from Troy

And they feasted nine days together
Menelaus, Helen, and Paris
And on the tenth day

Menelaus left for Crete
He had an appointment to keep
He needed to speak to a kinsman

Helen could rule his kingdom.
But that same night
Paris and Helen eloped

Taking treasures with them
And stole a quantity of gold
From Apollo's temple

At the first port of call
Helen gave herself to Paris
Then off they sailed again

Waves rose like walls
Some said it was Poseidon
Some said it was Athene in her fury

Some said it was Hera inflicting terror
But the couple survived
The mariners hugged the shore

Dropped anchor at Sidon
Where, in the banqueting hall,
To the astonishment of one and all

Never to be understood
Never to be accounted for
As if his mind were not his own

Paris killed the king
The king who had welcomed him
And took his treasure

His ships were already piled high
And they were piled higher
The Sidonians would never forget

They destroyed two ships
And would have destroyed more
But Paris escaped with his paramour

And the Sidonions were left
Aiming arrows from the shore
Wishing him death with every breath

As for the lovers, they sailed away
And after delays, they reached Troy.
The Trojans were enchanted from the start

They said Helen's beauty was divine
And so began days of roses and wine
But not for long

***

Agamemnon, of the House of Atreus,
Brother of Menelaus
Also rode the high seas

He was exacting levies
And planning a war
Reminding those chieftains

Who had wanted to marry Helen
Of the pledge they had made
And what they had bargained for

Standing on pieces of horse flesh
In the yard that ran with blood
Swearing to unite

And defend the rights
Of the suitor who was chosen
Should Helen of Sparta be stolen

And so the Trojan War began
Dark ships appeared in the harbor
Encampments rose outside the walls

The siege of Troy was underway
The gods of Olympus wanted more
Nothing pleased them like a war

But the Trojan War went on and on
No side winning
No side pulling ahead

Then Paris and Menelaus met face to face
The fighting stopped
The armies pulled back

'Let Menelaus and Paris fight it out'
Was the sentiment of one and all
Better that one should pay the cost

Than so many lives be lost
And what is more
It could bring an end to the war

Paris struck first
Menelaus drew his sword
But the gods intervened

They had already taken sides
They wanted to have their say
To have their say in their own way

Aphrodite wrapped Paris in a cloud
So he could not be seen
Menelaus, savagely roused, sniffed the ground

A rabid dog he might have been
But warriors of both sides sympathized
They sent scouts to rout him out

"Rout him out!" was the shout
But Paris could not be found
A crisis had been reached

Agamemnon stepped into the breach
Both armies waited on his word
"Menelaus is the victor," he declared

"The Trojans must give Helen back.
Then we can end this war."
Those were the words the warriors heard

But the gods intervened yet again
They didn't want peace; they wanted war
Pallas Athene came to the fore

She persuaded Pandarus
Who was a fool from the start
To shoot Menelaus through the heart

The truce was broken
Snapped like a twig in a dry season
The arrow glanced off

But what were the warriors to do
Except fight and fight some more
Fight as never before

Paris reappeared
He was ignored
Despised by Greek and Trojan

Even so, Paris shot the arrow
That killed Achilles
The greatest warrior of them all

Some said, the arrow was guided by Apollo
Whatever the case, Paris was not feted
His action was not celebrated

Though, for a time, he changed the war
Then Prince Philoctetes shot the arrows
That injured Paris

Three in all
That brought him close to death
And Paris begged to be taken

To the place he once called home
To the slopes of Mount Ida
Where he had been the chosen one

Of the lovely nymph Oenone
And they had hunted and herded together
Carved each other's names in beech and poplar

She knew the ways of prophecy taught by Rhea
And the ways of healing taught by Apollo
And they found her by the river

Oenone saw his plight
He asked her for his life
And she refused

She remembered his desertion
His long forgetfulness
She watched him die

Then killed herself
And the River Oeneus
Rose to claim her.

Hector, the Tamer of Horses

Achilles heart sunk in sorrow
At the sight of the suffering father

Offering his pleas on his knees--
A king in supplication

Come with barrows of treasure
Beseeching him for the body of Hector

The savage warrior's heart spoke for him:
"Evil is all men's lot, yet we must keep courage."

He told his slaves to bathe the body
Wrap it in soft purple

Wrap it round and round
So it would not be easily unbound

King Priam took his son away
Fighting stopped that very day

And for nine days after that
Each side respecting the other

Then they laid Hector on the pyre
And when all was burned

Libations quenched the fire
They put the bones into a golden urn

Set the urn into a hollow
Piled great stones on top

But the weeping did not stop
Such was the funeral of Hector

Beloved son of Priam
First-born of Hecube

Some said sired by Apollo
Such was the glory

Hector, the glorious one
Hector, the Tamer of Horses

Great Ajax Dishonored

The Trojan tide kept coming
Odysseus pushed it back
So he, Great Ajax, could retrieve

Achilles from the battlefield
Greatest warrior of them all
Fallen as his mother had foretold

The broadest, and the swiftest of the bold
And he, Great Ajax, only a step behind
Would shoulder the Great One

Carry the Great One home
Who better for the task than he?
A man must know his worth

And act accordingly
This was a day of destiny
That would go down in history

Great Ajax and Achilles together
Two cousins--it was meant to be
Moving as one over the battlefield

In the distance, Great Ajax saw
A tent flap open wide
Servants waiting inside

They had their spies
They were the first to know
They were waiting with the bier

Waiting for him
To bring the warrior home
And he was playing his part

He had heard the last gasp
He had thought it was his own
But it was the Fallen One's

The arrow had pierced his heel
Shot by Paris
Some said guided by Apollo

The lookout gave a shout
The servants all ran out
They would work together

As they should
He would bend at the knees
As best he could

So they could lift the Great One off
Lay him down
Then the rituals could start

For the servants, it was an art
But first, they brought a draught
For him to quench his thirst

Great Ajax saw the arms
Already under guard
The arms that would be his

Made for Achilles by Hephaestus
Arms like no other
Brought from Olympus by his mother

Dazzling and magical
A shield that seemed alive
As if the heat were still inside

The shield that would be his
As tradition had decreed
It was his due

To be received
By the one who retrieved
The warrior from the battlefield

It was the way it was done
He would be The One
The Honored One

He would take the shield with pride
It would never leave his side.
But when the hour came

And the leaders had convened
And Great Ajax stood so big and tall
A giant compared to one and all

The leaders passed him by
As if he were not there
They gave the arms to Odysseus

And he, Great Ajax stood
As if struck
By a mighty hand

One mightier than his own
He was locked in place
Unable to face

What had been done
He had been burnt, rent
And scored with claws

Only habit took him home
Where he lay
Hardening like clay

His life made small
His glory crushed
His honor stolen

He was the dishonored one
The arms had been awarded to another
Settled by secret ballot behind closed doors

Some said it was because Agamemnon
Hated the House of Aeacus
To which Great Ajax belonged

Some said it was because Agamemnon
Needed Odysseus; knew his cunning
At any crossroads, he was The One

But injustice had been done
A great man brought low
His honor taken

That same night
In his plight
Madness overtook him

He burst from his tent
Sword in hand
Ready to kill his enemies

Found them in a field eating grass
And felled them every one
"Agamemnon!" he shouted

"Menelaus!" he roared
And put them to the sword
Chained the surviving enemies together

Continued the slaughter
Hauled a huge Odysseus to his tent
Bound him to a tent-pole

Flogged him with a horse's halter
Until he faltered
And he, Great Ajax, fell

Found himself on the floor
With a thirst so big
He could drink from the Styx

Then he saw the gore
A ram bound and tied
Eyes, gouged, and on the floor

Panic seized him
Sent him from his tent
What he saw

Nothing had prepared him for
He sank to his knees
Dead and dying cattle in the field

Mutilated sheep
His own bloodied sword
He had been dishonored before

Now he was dishonored more
He knew what course to take
He left a message for his son

To take his shield
Made from seven bulls' hides
The shield that once had satisfied

Why would he even want another?
He called on Zeus
To tell his brother

Where to find the corpse
He called on Hermes
To conduct his soul

To the Fields of Asphodel
He called on the Erinnyes
To avenge his death

For the injustice done
And he fell on his sword
But the sword buckled

Taking the shape of a bow
He remembered the charm
Cast by Heracles:

His skin could not be pierced
Except for the armpit
And a place in the neck

Where in the neck he did not know
But he tried and tried again
And was found at dawn

Teucer, his half-brother, found him
And tore out his hair
His father would blame him

He would accuse him of neglect
Thinking of Telamon, his father,
Teucer fell on his knees and wept

He knew the score
He would have a family no more
He would never be allowed ashore

Menelaus came by
He wanted the body left exposed
Allowed to decompose

Picked at by kites and vultures
Teucer, the greatest archer in all Greece,
Sent the boar home and would have killed him

Had Odysseus not come by
And offered his condolences
He was a different kind of man

He negotiated with Agamemnon
To allow Great Ajax a suicide's coffin
And to be buried in the ground

Since a pyre and urn were not allowed
He offered to help with the rites
Teucer heard words of mercy

Thanked him for his courtesy
But declined the offer
Said it was a family matter

In the end, when all was said and done
Odysseus gave the arms to Achilles' son
And everyone agreed Neoptolemus should be the one.

Palamedes

Palamedes had a mind beyond the reach of most men
He invented dice that took up time when time was slack
It was a game warriors played while waiting

He invented lighthouses that prevented ships
From being tossed on the rocks
And lost

He invented scales and measures
Which eased methods of exchange
With all the reasoning it entailed

He had command of an alphabet
Could read and write
He was a man given to thinking

And figuring
Valued by king and country
A man set apart from the start

But he needed a signal
A sentinel on guard at his side
Because he was not mindful

Of other men's pride
Knew not what that could lead to
Truth was: Palamedes made adversaries

***

Achilles had taken cities allied to Troy
Killed kings and taken spoils
Great Ajax had done the same

Warriors had fallen in the dust
Pyres were burning day and night
The tenth year was approaching

Agamemnon was making the final thrust
He had amassed armies before Troy
And was in need of supplies

They had foraged the coast of Asia Minor
Now he was thinking of Thrace
That Thrace would be the place

He sent Odysseus to find grain
He sent the Resourceful One
The one he could count on

But Odysseus came back empty-handed
Unusual for him
His ship was a hull with nothing in it

Nobody thought to blame him
Except one who knew no better
His name was Palamedes

He stepped out of a circle of men
And before a gathering
Excoriated the chieftain

Called him a "sloth" and a "coward"
"There was no corn!" Odysseus said.
But he was shocked

He had heard words
Never before used against him
If he had been Achilles

He would have run him through
If he'd been Great Ajax
He would have punched him

And that alone would do
"If you had gone in my stead
"You'd have done no better!" he said

Palamedes took that as a challenge
Next morning, he set sail for Thrace
And returned with a ship piled high

Corn for everyone
It was a welcome sight
Palamedes was a hero for a day and a night

But he maintained for everyone to hear
That the shipload of grain was easily obtained
"How could anyone not find it?"

Odysseus appeared sanguine
But his manly pride was hurt
He remembered ten years before

When a dark ship came to his shore
And three men came walking
He had grabbed a peasant's hat

Feigned madness
He did not want to go to war
He recalled that Palamedes was the one

Who had thrown his little son before the plow
How certain had he been of his disguise?
That it was a ruse?

What if he, Odysseus, had truly lost his mind?
Had not turned the plow aside
And his little son had died?

What then would have been his excuse?
The words “sloth” and “coward” stuck in his craw
The insult could not stand

During torturous days and torturous nights
With his rage concealed, but gleaming white
Odysseus laid his plan

He sent word to Agamemnon:
He’d had a dream sent by the gods
Telling him treachery was afoot

The camp must be moved for a day and a night
Agamemnon heard the words
Odysseus was so often right; he was The One

The king gave orders: the camp was moved
That night, when the work was completed
And men and animals were depleted

And the sounds of sleep rang loud
Odysseus buried a sack full of gold
In that place where Palamedes tent had been

Then he directed a Phrygian prisoner to write a letter
It said, 'From Priam to Palemedes:
The gold is your price for betraying the Greeks.'

He ordered the prisoner to take the letter to Palamedes
The prisoner was killed along the way
Next day, he was found, a letter in his hand

The letter was taken to the king
Palamedes was seized directly
Accused of treachery

Odysseus suggested Palamedes' tent be searched
Also the ground that had been uncovered …
And the sack of gold was discovered

Palamedes was led to the stoning place
"He's a traitor," Agamemnon said
"What has to be done … has to be done."

And as the sun was rising
The warriors stoned him, every one
Stoned him until the end had come

Palamedes' last words passed to posterity
Down the tortuous corridors of history:
"Truth … you have predeceased me!"

The Wooden Horse

None had been able to do it
Not savage Achilles
Greatest warrior of them all

Not Antilochus, old Nestor's son
Patroclus was dead
Ajax was dishonored

The gods had taken sides
They watched avidly from the skies
Nothing pleased them like a war

A thousand ships along the shore
Survivors fighting as never before
But nothing could bring down Troy

The captured prophet Helenus
Said, Go to the Isle of Lemnos
Get the bow and arrows of Heracles

These were obtained, but nothing changed
And nothing could be expected to change
While Troy was still protected

A suggestion was made:
"Take Athene's image
Seize the Palladium!"

Odysseus and Diomedes heard the words.
That night, they searched the wall
For the part built by Aeacus of Locris

Little Ajax told the chieftains what he knew
The weakest part was where the fig tree grew
They found the culvert

Where the snake had passed through
And that was what the chieftains had to do
Pass through the culvert without shield or sword

Follow the shadow of the wall
Find the citadel
Enter the hall

Grab the legless Palladium
An image three cubits high
Carved in memory of Pallas, a childhood friend

Then with Athene's sacred image stolen
The Greeks felt emboldened
But not for long

The stalemate dragged on
Again, Odysseus stepped up to the plate
His resourceful mind at work, and he said:

We will build a horse
One made of wood
Huge in dimensions

Hollow inside
Where chieftains could hide
To be placed outside

The Scaean Gates of Troy.
The craftsmen complied
They worked day and night

Using wood from ships on the shore
And when the work was done
The Greeks were gone

They took their ships behind some islands
That rose up from the sea
Affording invisibility

Dear Reader: The following hours
Would go down in infamy
Never to be forgotten in history.

***

At first light, Trojan watchers on the wall
Saw what ten years of watching
Had not prepared them for:

An empty harbor …
But they knew eyes could deceive
And gods were known to tease

They exclaimed, and looked again
It seemed the Greeks had gone
The harbor was empty as a drum

People came out of their houses
Not yet ready to shout for joy
They flocked to the places

Where the camps had been
Examined places never seen
They gaped at the wooden horse

What did it mean?
Why was it there?
Was it a sign of some kind?

Then the lone Greek left behind
Came out of his hiding place
And was seized

Weeping and protesting
He was dragged before the king
In truth, he was dissembling

Schooled as he was by Odysseus
To play a role
He said his countrymen

Had marked him out for sacrifice
He had taken flight
Hidden in a swamp

Almost drowned
Barely able to breathe
Waiting for the ships to leave

King Priam looked at the man
Showing signs of mud and waterweed
And was inclined to believe …

He asked about the wooden horse
The Greek said: If the horse were burned
Pallas Athene would feel spurned

And that same god, in her wrath,
Would do, what his countrymen
Had failed to do--destroy Troy

On the other hand,
If the gates of Troy were opened wide
And the great horse taken inside

And placed before the citadel
Pallas Athene would be pleased
She would no longer feel aggrieved

Cassandra demurred
But no one heard
She took herself away

But a priest would stay
With his two sons
To make the case

To leave the horse
Outside the gates
"Don't let it in!"

"They want us dead
Beware of Greeks bearing gifts," he said.
And it so happened

In the dungeons of the deep
That Poseidon heard those fateful words
And was filled with rage

A rage not easily explained
Not easily assuaged
But Poseidon wanted to have his say:

He sent two serpents
Gliding over the sea
To crush the life

Out of priest and progeny
To coil them around
Until they made no sound

And lay dead on the ground
So witnesses could see
The power of his sovereignty

And know they were bound
To the Lord and Ruler of the Sea
And people would know

What course to take
And what would happen
If they made a mistake

People went to their king
Conferred with him
They opened the Scaean Gates of Troy

And let the wooden horse in
Hauled it to its place
Before Athene's citadel

Where it would remain
In its true domain
Bringing favor once again

***

And the people were relieved
Thought the god would be appeased
Women gathered flowers

Garlanded its mane
Placed roses at its hoofs
And the bard sang again

Of health, wealth and happiness
Paeans to a Trojan king
Who said the revelry would begin

But first a night of rest was needed
Because a ten year siege had ended
And there would be days of feasting

Garlanded girls dancing
Voices raised in song
Stirring tales of glory told

Of Hector the Magnificent
Of heroes young and bold
And there would be no more weeping

Because the Greeks had gone
And we the Trojan people
Had gloriously won

So looking once more over the wall
And seeing no sign of life at all
No ships in the harbor

No ships along the shore
People went home in relief
To a deep abiding sleep

***

Under a starlit sky
The chieftains of the horse emerged
Men who had been confined

They opened the Scaean Gates of Troy
Let the Greeks, who had returned, inside
They ran through the town

Entered the unguarded houses
Slit the throats of sleeping people
Gained an advantage

Torched the houses
Set the city ablaze
None to be saved

That was the injunction
The chieftains gave
Everything to dust

Bodies to be crushed
All the buildings burned
Glory must be earned

King Priam to be killed
Hecube saved to be enslaved
Others set aside as concubines

And the children
Defiled, stolen, traded
Sacrificed and degraded

We know Polyxena
Hecube's daughter was slaughtered
On Achilles' grave

We know Hector's son
So small and young
Was thrown from the Trojan wall

Troy was a massacre, an abattoir
Trojans were caught unawares
And none were spared

Except those whom Aphrodite saved:
Helen, who some say caused the war
Aeneas, his father, and his child

Then when all was destroyed
Greeks ran through the gore
Made for their ships as never before

And when they looked back
They saw a city sacked
Like a warrior brought to his knees

When the last blow has been struck
And his head falls in the dust
But it was not for them to wonder why

It was a case of do or die
They saw the vultures in the sky
Smelled the flesh of man and beast

Knew the destruction was complete
And the dark ships moved from shore
Some said the wooden horse won the war.

Orestes

Orestes' fate hung on a sword's edge
He needed to avenge his father's death
But there were two who killed …

He could kill the one
But could he kill the other
When the other was his mother?

He consulted the Delphic Oracle
Apollo urged him on
He said: The House of Atreus is ill fated

It needs to be cleansed and expiated
He would be an outcast of society
Debarred from shrine and temple

Afflicted with leprosy that ate his flesh
Unless he avenged his father's death
And killed "the two who slew."

Those were Apollo's words
And, according to Apollo
They were Zeus's too

So what was he to do?
He could slay Aegisthus
Run him through

He was his father's murderer
The usurper of his throne
Who rode in his chariot

Wielded his scepter
Walked in his robes
Stole his gold

And slept in his bed …
Killing him was easily done
But killing his mother was another matter

Matricide
Was a crime like no other
A crime against god and man

***

He had heard from the Silent One
The One who Watched and Served
That the king lived in fear

Aegisthus spoke of a young man
Who would come into view
Step from the shadows

Stand at the end of the wall
Vanish down the hall
Reappear in silhouette

Pass behind the throne
Breathe on his neck
While he slept

Aegisthus knew
Orestes would come
It was the obligation of a son

He offered gold for his assassination
Paid a man to watch the shore
He sat on Agamemnon's throne

But it did not feel like his own
And it was not his own
Truth was Clytemnestra ruled

She felt no whips or stings
She was not the restless one
She did not turn and turn about

Like a dog before he sleeps
She had avenged Iphigenia's death
And the baby killed at her breast

She had done what she had to do
She had slain the one who slew
And she had three more children to consider

But the Silent One who Watched and Served
Told Orestes there was more:
His sister had been cast out

People hung their heads in shame
Electra was the leading princess of Mycenae
Princes had contended for her hand

They had all been banned
The king and queen had married her to another
A peasant taken from the fields

The peasant viewed the wedding with suspicion
He thought the sport was of a savage kind
He vacated his hovel

He would not stand accused
But he brought the princess food
Installed strong bolts

Fortified her door
He, and the people of Mycenae
Thought a princess should have more

But Electra's defiant spirit was strong
She still called out the offensive truth:
"Adulterers! Murderers!" she shouted

Mycenae turned the other cheek
But Aegisthus wanted her dead
Clytemnestra said:

"She has been cast out
Married to a peasant
Isn't that enough?"

But that wasn't enough
Aegisthus wanted more
He galloped his horse past her door

He was thinking of a dungeon in a distant city
Where she would never see the light of day
Where a princess in rags would hold no sway

But Electra's spirit refused to die
She knew her brother would come
He would come as the avenging son

He would kill the murderers, one and two
It was what he was fated to do
He would come and see it through

She would walk in the fragrant hills
Pray for her brother's return
And at the going down of the sun

She would kneel at her father's tomb
Pour a libation
Ask Zeus for her father's salvation

***

As a boy Orestes had been taken
To his uncle's house
Strophius was his name

He had a happy childhood
But the child became a man
It was then he learned

That his fate was sealed
That there was no appeal
His father had been murdered

His death had to be avenged
His tutor had said:
"Your father was buried without ceremony

"No libations and no myrtle-boughs
People were forbidden to attend
That was the shame of Agamemnon's end.

"Appease the angry dead," the old man begged.
Orestes walked in the shadows
Turned in anguish to the Silent One:

"What has my family done?
Why is Apollo so angry?
Why is the House of Atreus ill fated?

"Why is it defiled?
What was the terrible sin?
When did it begin?"

The One who Watched and Served
Preferred the Silent Way
But he surrendered

His voice came from afar:
It began with Tantalus, he said
Who, of all Zeus's mortal sons

Was the only one
To dine with the gods
Eat the nectar and ambrosia

Play in the golden palace
Roll his ball along the floor
Take turns among the urns

But as Tantalus grew
He grew to hate the gods
And his hate kept growing

It was a hate that made him tremble
Prevailed upon his mind
Wrested judgment from him

He wanted to demean them
Attack their overweening pride
And with the march of time

The seeds of hate multiplied
The Silent One stopped
He preferred the Silent Way

But he heard Orestes say:
"I have to know! I have to know!
Help me! Help me!"

The Silent One prayed for fortitude
He breathed deeply and continued:
When Tantalus became King of Lydia

He saw his chance
He would provide a banquet
The gods would condescend to come

He would sacrifice his only son
Throw him in a boiling cauldron
Serve the gods a mortal dish

Tell them to their horror
When it was all over.
A gong sounded

"I have given you the beginning only …"
Were the words Orestes heard
And the Silent One was gone

Orestes was alone
Sitting on his rock staring out to sea
He had been warned about the Erinnyes

Black shapes with hair like snakes
The Pythoness in the temple
Had given him a bow of horn

To repel the Dreaded Ones
It would send them back, she said
Were they to attack

Orestes sought out Pylades
His cousin, and his friend
Told him what the Oracle had said:

"Slay the two who slew.
Atone for death by death.
Shed blood for old blood shed."

Pylades told Orestes he was not alone
They had been boyhood friends
They would be friends to the end.

***

But Orestes knew
The story of his House was not yet told
He knew the beginning only

When the sun rose
He went to his rock
And called the Silent One

The voice came in bursts
With the blowing of the wind
In gusts, then all in a rush

The story began where it had left off:
Tantalus set out the mortal dish
But the gods knew what he had done

He was doomed to a pool in Hades
Where he could never satisfy his thirst
He would bend his parched throat to the water

And the water would soak into the ground
He would stretch mightily with his neck
Towards the fruit that brushed his cheek

And the fruit would rise out of reach
But his son, Pelops,
The gods restored to wholeness

Except for a shoulder, made of ivory
And Pelops grew and prospered
He married the Princess Hippodameia

He had contended for her hand
And they had two sons:
Atreus and Thyestes

Fond brothers both
Who faced the world together
Pledged loyalty to each other

Chose their wives
Were blessed with children
And the sounds of children playing

But then, one day, the curse of the House of Atreus
Re-emerged, rose up dark and heavy from a swamp
Broke the surface without a head

As if returned from the dead:
Thyestes betrayed his brother
Seduced his brother's wife

The curse of Atreus was alive in the palace
Cracks were heard
And the falling of rocks

Loyalties had been traded for lust
Hopes and dreams turned to dust
Love replaced with hate and rage

The sounds Atreus made
Came from someone deranged
Servants and children were running

As if trapped in a cage
With an animal
Both dangerous and suffering

For Atreus, it was a crime like no other
Betrayed by his own brother
And he wanted his brother to suffer

He wanted his brother's suffering
To be greater than his own
He grasped at the air

His knuckles keen and white
He walked stiff-legged along the walls
What could he do?

What punishment could he devise?
Then he saw his brother's children playing
He seized them both

He cut them limb from limb
Served them up to their father
Cooked and plattered

Thyestes ate his fill
Then he heard the words
No man should hear

The words that made him ill
He had eaten the ones he loved
The ones he held most dear

He wanted no one to come near
He writhed on the floor
His agony bound to him

Lashed like rope around him
Pulled tight, never to be eased
Never to be undone

But it wasn't the end
The brothers died as all men do
But Thyestes died unavenged

So the duty passed to his son, the little one,
Who had been too small to play by the wall
And his name was Aegisthus

Atreus, the king, was dead
So he killed the son instead
His name was Agamemnon

The Silent One was gone
Orestes' knew there was no appeal
Knew his fate was sealed.

***

The young men journeyed to Mycenae
Sought out Agamemnon's tomb
And found a woman kneeling there

Electra looked up
She saw the brother she had waited for
Noted the cloak worked by her hand

Noted the scar on his forehead
But she needed no proof, and she wept
She had been bereft of love so long

"Your face is my father's face," she said
And Orestes claimed her for his sister
And introduced her to Pylades

Who, as it happened,
Would be with her in the future
But Orestes was full of dread

He remembered what the tutor had said:
"Clytemnestra threw a garment over his head
Made of netting, with no neck or sleeves

"Aegisthus stabbed him with his sword
Agamemnon fell back
And Clytemnestra . . . "

Orestes took himself in hand
He was the one who wanted them dead
Electra must hide

The two men would go inside
They strode to the palace gate
Pylades carrying a brazen urn

They said they were messengers
Bearing bad news from Strophius
"Orestes is dead," they said

"What were they to do with the ashes?
What were the instructions?"
The tale rang true

The gates were opened
The guards stepped aside
The men went inside

No sooner in
Than Orestes slew the one
Then slew the other

And the other was his mother
And he and Pylades, together
Killed the offspring, one and all

Then Orestes fled
Now he was the guilty one
Now he was the ruined one

Outside, the servants gathered
They looked on him favorably
They would transfer their loyalty

They knew why he had come
He was the dutiful son
And they were his servants too

But behind the servants
The Erinnyes gathered
Black shapes with hair like snakes

The servants said no one was there
"It's your fancy, Orestes! Stay!"
But he fled away

Fled from the palace where the bodies lay
Left Pylades and Electra
He had committed a crime like no other

A crime against god and man
And so Orestes' wandering began
The Erinnyes followed

He saw their shapes and their bleeding eyes
The bow of horn did not protect him
The Silent One who Watched and Served

Sent word. His voice was sad and gentle
He said Pylades and Electra were betrothed
And Orestes was consoled

But he walked on
Not thinking of the years
Or the changes wrought in him

Then one day after all his wandering
Meeting the good people, and the bad
Seeking shelter from the desert sand

Tasting the fruits of the fertile land
Where the river overflowed
And the jewels of the earth shone like gold

He came, again, to the islands that he knew
He sat on his rock, and stared out to sea
Across the water was the great city

He glanced behind
The Erinnyes were still there
The Dreaded Ones had never left him

But he would go to Athens
He would seek out Apollo
Apollo spoke of absolution

He urged him to go before the tribunal
To stand before Athene who was the judge
He said he would speak on his behalf

He was the one who had prevailed upon him
Urged him to kill
Exhorted him from the start

He would play his part
Judge Athene listened to Apollo's words
Heard what Orestes had to say

She said: "The guilt of Atreus is expiated
The House of Atreus is no longer defiled
Orestes of the House of Atreus

Is absolved of all his crimes."
Orestes glanced behind
The Dreaded Ones fled before his eyes.

Notes on Pronunciation

The Greek names found in the text and transcribed below into a phonetic system may help the reader with pronunciation. One key feature is that all vowels are sounded (for example, 'e' is not mute at the end of a word). The meanings of the names (taken from Graves's *The Greek Myths II*) are given in brackets.

Achilles	a kil leez	(lipless)
Aeacus	ay ah kus	(bewailing, or earth-born)
Aegisthus	ay gist hus	(goat strength)
Ajax	ay jaks	(of the earth)
Aphrodite	af ro di tee	(foam-born)
Ares	ah reez	(male warrior)
Athene	a thee nee	Sumerian (Queen of Heaven)
Atreus	at roos	(fearless)
Cheiron	ki ron	(hand)
Diomedes	di om eed eez	(god-like cunning of Argos)
Erinnyes	e rin yeez	(angry ones)
Eurynome	yoor ee no mee	(wide wandering, or wide rule)
Hephaestus	hee fes tus	(he who shines by day)
Hera	hee rah	(protectress)
Heracles	hee rah kleez	(glory of Hera)
Hermes	her meez	(cairn, or pillar)
Io	i oh	(moon)
Iphigeneia	if ig een e ya	(mothering a strong race)
Lycomedes	li ko mee deez	(wolf-cunning)
Neoptolemus	nee op tol ee mus	(new war)
Nereids	ner ee idz	(wet ones)
Odysseus	oh dis see us	(angry)
Oenone	ee no nee	(queen of wine)
Oeneus	ee noos	(vinous)
Orestes	o res teez	(mountaineer)
Palamedes	pal am eed eez	(ancient wisdom)
Penelope	pe nel o pee	(striped duck)
Pleiades	plee ya deez	(sailing ones, or flock of doves)
Telamon	tel a mon	(he who suffers, or supports)
Teucer	too ker	(teucter, artisan)
Thetis	thee tis	(disposer)
Thyestes	thee es teez	(pestle)
Zeus	(as in 'loose')	(bright sky)

Maps of Real Places

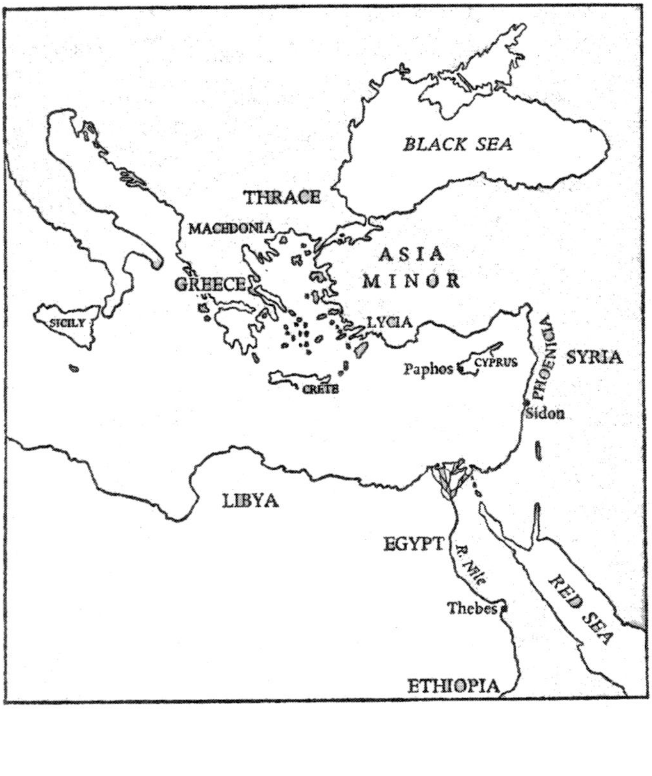

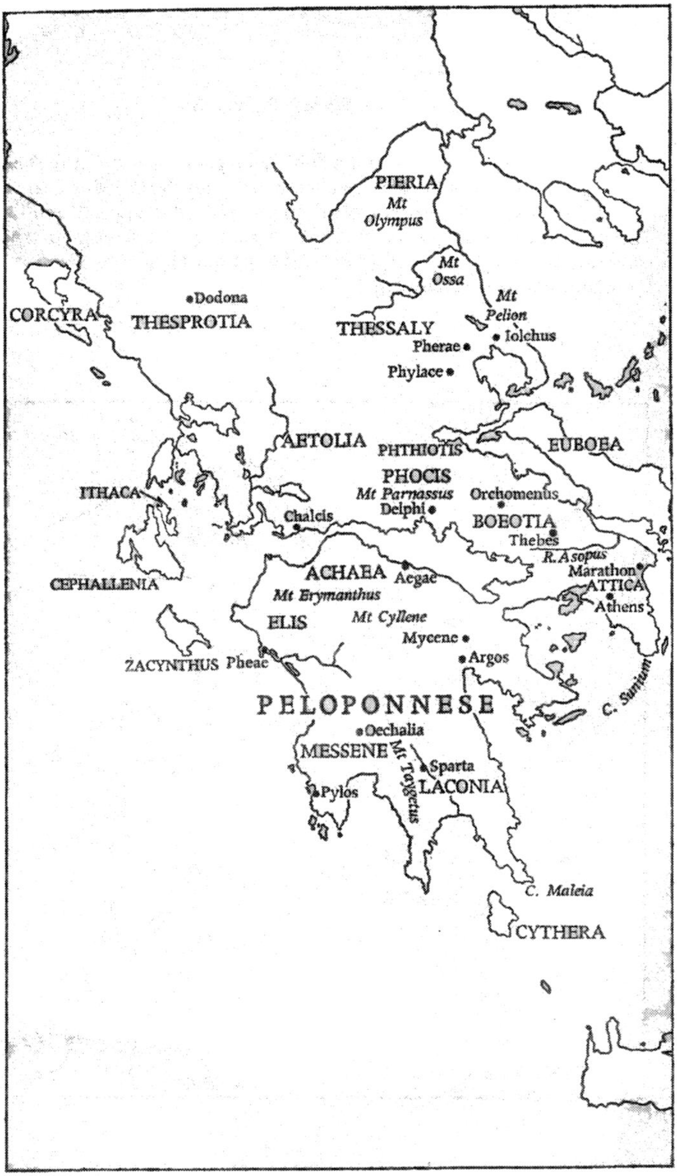
PIERIA
Mt Olympus
Mt Ossa
Mt Pelion
Dodona
CORCYRA
THESPROTIA
THESSALY
Pherae
Iolchus
Phylace
AETOLIA
PHTHIOTIS
EUBOEA
PHOCIS
ITHACA
Mt Parnassus
Orchomenus
Delphi
Chalcis
BOEOTIA
Thebes
R. Asopus
ACHAEA
Aegae
Marathon
ATTICA
CEPHALLENIA
Mt Erymanthus
Athens
ELIS
Mt Cyllene
Mycene
Argos
ZACYNTHUS
Pheae
C. Sunium
PELOPONNESE
Oechalia
MESSENE
Mt Taygetus
Sparta
Pylos
LACONIA
C. Maleia
CYTHERA

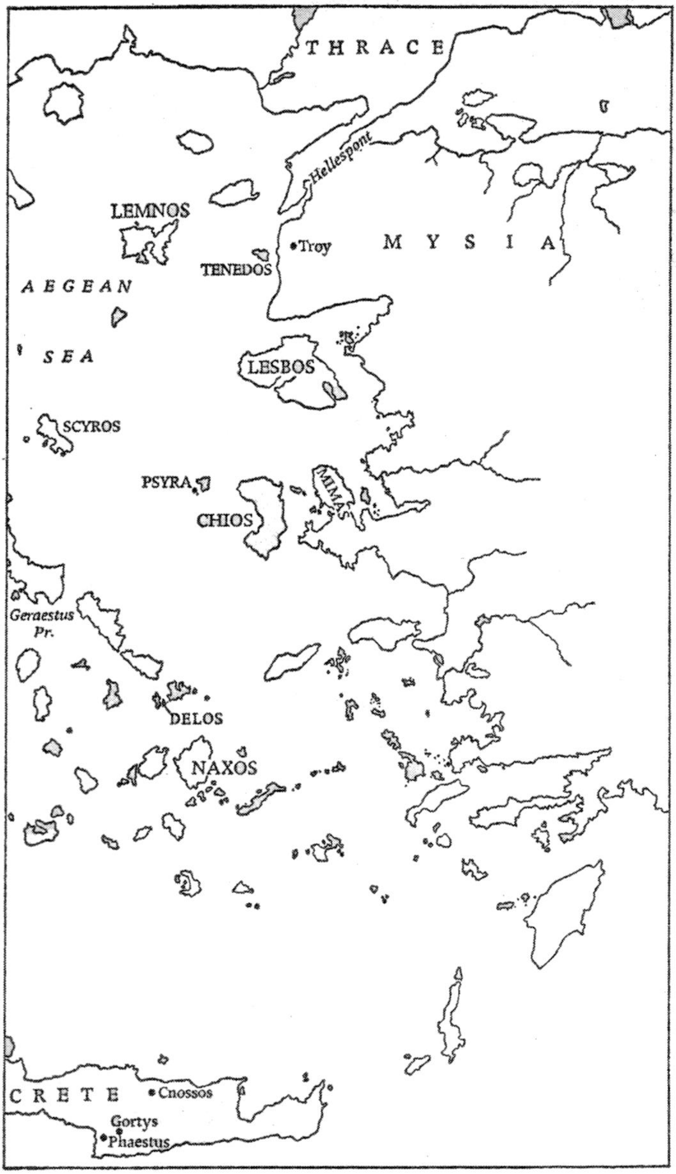
THRACE
Hellespont
LEMNOS
Troy
MYSIA
TENEDOS
AEGEAN
SEA
LESBOS
SCYROS
PSYRA
MIMAS
CHIOS
Geraestus
Pr.
DELOS
NAXOS
CRETE
Cnossos
Gortys
Phaestus

CPSIA information can be obtained
at www.ICGtesting.com
Printed in the USA
LVOW11*2136181217
560162LV00001B/12/P

9 780981 330631